YOUR POLLINATORS

TIM HARRIS

KNOW
YOUR
POLLINATORS

TIM HARRIS

Old Pond
PUBLISHING

Know Your Pollinators

Old Pond Publishing is an imprint of Fox Chapel Publishers International Ltd.

Edited and designed by D & N Publishing, Wiltshire, UK

ISBN 978-1-91215-855-3

A catalogue record for this book is available from the British Library.

Fox Chapel Publishing
903 Square Street
Mount Joy, PA 17552

Fox Chapel Publishers International Ltd.
7 Danefield Road, Selsey (Chichester)
West Sussex PO20 9DA, U.K.

www.oldpond.com

We are always looking for talented authors. To submit an idea, please send a brief inquiry to acquisitions@foxchapelpublishing.com.

Printed and bound in Malaysia
10 9 8 7 6 5 4 3 2 1

Front cover photos, from left to right: Honeybee, lime butterfly, and seven-spotted ladybug.
Back cover photos, from left to right: Bumblebee, seven-spotted ladybug, painted lady, and hornet mimic hoverfly.

Contents

Foreword

The primary way in which plants create new generations is by producing seeds containing all the genetic information necessary to grow a new plant. Seeds are made when pollen is transferred from the stamen of one plant to the stigma of another, fertilizing it. This may be done by the wind, by water, or by animals. The animals responsible for this incredibly important transfer are called pollinators. They include bats and hummingbirds, but it is the insect pollinators that are the subject of this book: bees, butterflies, moths, hoverflies, and beetles. As well as being real heroes of the natural world, all are beautiful in their own way, and many can be attracted to your garden or backyard.

*(opposite) Monarch butterfly (*Danaus plexippus*) on thistle.*

BEES AND WASPS

Bees are pollinators par excellence. More than 20,000 different kinds are known. Most visit flowers to suck up energy-giving nectar. Pollen—essential for the raising of young—attaches to a bee's body as it moves from plant to plant. Some are more efficient pollen collectors than others. For example, hairy bumblebees have pollen-gathering "brushes" on various parts of their bodies. In moving from plant to plant, bees transfer pollen from the stamen of one flower to the stigma of the next, enabling pollination. Most of the pollen is taken back to the colony or the nest burrow to feed young bees.

The range of bee lifestyles is truly bewildering. In social species such as honeybees, female "workers" perform most of a colony's important functions. There is a clear differentiation between breeding queens, nonbreeding workers, and male drones. The workers make honey from nectar, pollen, and enzymes produced in their stomach, and this provides food during the winter, when nectar and pollen are unavailable.

Most bees are solitary, however, with a single female establishing a nest and laying eggs. And still more bees are kleptoparasites, breaking into the nests of other bees to lay their own eggs inside. Closely related, wasps are predatory insects but since they also visit flowers, they are pollinators too.

*(opposite) Buff-tailed bumblebee (*Bombus terrestris) *covered with pollen.*

1

Bombus terrestris

Buff-tailed Bumblebee

Characteristics

Length: Queen 0.71 in (18 mm); worker and male 0.51–0.55 in (13–14 mm).
Flight season: May–October.
Nectar sources: Very varied.
Habitat: Meadows, farmland, parks, gardens.

The large, furry, European bumblebee is a familiar sight as it forages on garden flowers. It can be identified by two orange "collars" on a black background, one near the neck and one on the abdomen. The tip of the abdomen is buff in queens and males, but whitish in workers.

After emerging from hibernation in spring, a queen will start foraging busily on flowers such as sallows, plums, cherries, and gorse—and she will pick an underground site for a new colony, often an old mouse nest. Once settled, she lays eggs, which hatch into larvae. When it reaches its peak, there may be more than 500 bees in a colony, most of them workers (all females), which perform most of its important functions: foraging for food at flowers as varied as knapweeds, daisies, lavender, deadnettles, and ivy, according to the season. The workers also defend the nest from attackers and care for the larvae. Male bees, or drones, hatch from unfertilized eggs; they leave the colony when they reach adulthood to go in search of a mate, their only function.

2

Characteristics

Length: Queen 0.67–
0.82 in (17–21 mm);
worker and male
0.39–0.67 in (10–17 mm).
Flight season:
April–November.
Nectar sources:
Very varied.
Habitat: Forest, farmland,
parks, gardens.

Bombus impatiens

Eastern Bumblebee

This is one of North America's most important pollinators. Abundant in the east, it is now used for greenhouse pollination in California and Mexico, far outside its natural range. It is a social insect. Workers fly from flower to flower to collect pollen; goldenrods are particularly popular nectar sources, along with thistles, apples, clovers, vetches, burdocks, rhododendrons, and tomatoes. Some pollen becomes attached to the bees' hairy bodies and some is collected in "pollen baskets" on the legs. The workers take it back to the underground nest, which typically houses 300–500 bees.

Eastern bumblebees are mostly covered in black hairs, with a band of yellow on the thorax and another on the first segment of the abdomen. Queens emerge from hibernation in March or April and fly in search of sites for new colonies, which are typically established in May. Each queen lays around 2,000 eggs in a season, about half of them surviving to adulthood. Female workers emerge in June, then the males and new queens appear in August and September. In late fall, the old queen and the workers die, as do the males, although not before mating with the next generation of queens.

Characteristics
Length: Queen 0.82–
0.90 in (21–23 mm);
worker and male
0.39–0.75 in (10–19 mm).
Flight season:
April–September.
Nectar sources:
Very varied.
Habitat: Meadows,
farmland, parks, gardens.

3

Bombus griseocollis

Brown-belted Bumblebee

A frequent visitor to coneflowers, milkweeds, clovers, vetches, peas, and beans, the North American brown-belted bumblebee is a generalist forager. Common east of the Rockies, its range also extends to Oregon and northern California. It can thrive anywhere there are flowers—even in the middle of the largest cities. A male was once seen 102 floors up on the Empire State Building in New York. The brown-belted bumblebee emerges later and becomes inactive later in the year than its eastern bumblebee counterpart. Its head and thorax are mostly black, with some yellow hairs, and the abdomen is yellow, banded black. Workers usually have a brown "belt" around the abdomen.

Brown-belted bumblebees live in relatively small colonies, usually with fewer than 50 workers. As with other eusocial bees, there is a clear division of labour within the colony, with the queen laying the eggs and the workers doing most of the chores. Unusually, however, the males—whose primary function is to mate with young queens—help incubate the pupae.

4

Apis mellifera

Western Honeybee

Characteristics

Length: Queen 0.70–
0.79 in (18–20 mm);
worker 0.35–0.39 in
(9–10 mm); male 0.47–
0.51 in (12–13 mm).
Flight season: Mostly
March–October.
Nectar sources:
Very varied.
Habitat: Meadows,
farmland, woodland,
parks, gardens.

Yellowish-buff, with dark bands on the abdomen, this bee probably originated in Africa and was one of the first insects to be domesticated, around 9,000 years ago. Honeybees were taken to North America in 1622 and now live on every continent apart from Antarctica. Most are kept in artificial hives, from which honey and wax combs are harvested. Hives are taken to areas where orchards require pollination.

Unlike most bees, its colonies may persist for several years, and queens can live to eight years of age. If a colony becomes too large, its old queen and many of its workers may "swarm" in spring—leaving the nest en masse to relocate. If this happens, the new queens that emerge fight for dominance.

Colonies may hold up to 80,000 bees, mostly workers that secrete wax to build the hive, clean and guard the nest, raise the young, and forage for nectar and pollen. Workers can communicate the location of good sources of nectar by performing a figure-eight dance. Once the nectar is brought back to the nest, it is converted into honey to feed the colony, and the pollen collected in the workers' "bee baskets" is used to make "bee bread" to feed the young.

5

Characteristics

Length: 0.51–0.63 in
(13–16 mm).
Flight season: March–May.
Nectar sources: Blueberries.
Habitat: Swamps,
cultivation, gardens.

Habropoda laboriosa

Blueberry Digger

The North American blueberry digger is only active for a short time each spring. Blueberry cultivation largely depends on this dark bee, which emerges just before the blueberries come into flower. These are solitary, ground-nesting bees. Females dig burrows in loose, sandy soil, and the larvae that emerge from their eggs feed on pollen and nectar left by the mother. They pupate, then emerge the following spring. Newly emerged males are sometimes so keen to find mates that they dig into the ground to find the females before they have emerged!

Although active for just three to five weeks, each female is believed to visit about 50,000 flowers during her short life, pollinating enough of them to produce 6,000 blueberries. The only way pollen can exit the plant's stamen is from a small opening in the top, and then only when it is shaken. The secret of the blueberry digger's success is that it latches on to the stamen and rapidly vibrates its flight muscles. This action shakes out the pollen, some of which attaches to the hairy bee and later sticks to the stigma of the next flower visited. Such "buzz pollination" is only practiced by some bees. Bumblebees can also do it, but they don't emerge until later in the spring.

6

Characteristics

Length: 0.79–0.87 in (20–22 mm).

Flight season: Late February–June.

Nectar sources: Spring-blossoming flowers and shrubs, lavender, sweet peas, wisteria.

Habitat: Grassland, scrub, orchards, vineyards, gardens.

Xylocopa violacea

Violet Carpenter Bee

This glossy black bee, with a sparse covering of hairs and violet wings, is one of Europe's largest. The female's habit of boring into dead wood to create a nest gives this species its name. These bees hibernate over winter and emerge in late winter or early spring to search for mates. After mating, the female looks for a nest site; when she has found some suitable dead wood, she excavates a tunnel in it. Her jaws can burrow in sound as well as rotten wood. She lays between three and thirty eggs in small cells. When the larvae hatch, she places a ball of pollen beside each for them to feed on. The next generation of adults emerges in late summer.

Despite its large size, and the disconcerting buzz of its wings, the violet carpenter bee is not aggressive, and only stings as a last resort. The bee's liking for wooden pallets as nest sites has helped it colonize new areas in recent years, and it is spreading north in Europe, doubtless helped by climate change.

7

Characteristics

Length: 0.75–0.90 in
(19–23 mm).
Flight season:
March–October.
Nectar sources: Many,
including fruit trees.
Habitat: Woodland,
farmland, gardens, parks.

Xylocopa virginica

Eastern Carpenter Bee

North America's most familiar carpenter bee is an important pollinator of fruit trees and other crops. It has a black head and abdomen with short yellow hairs on the thorax; the sexes look similar but males have a patch of yellow hair on their faces. The eastern carpenter bee is unusual in several respects. It is neither a solitary species nor is it truly social. Small clusters of nest holes are often found close to each other in wood. The female uses her strong jaws to dig a hole in which to lay her eggs, and sometimes one nest hole will branch into several different burrows, each housing a different female. Any dead wood will serve as a nest site but cut cedar and pine are popular, and sometimes these bees excavate in wooden buildings or furniture.

Although it is an important pollinator, visiting a wide variety of flowers, this bee is sometimes a "nectar robber," using its maxillae to split open the corolla tube of a flower to reach its nectary—meaning it doesn't brush past the flower's stamens and pick up pollen.

8

Characteristics

Length: 0.31–0.39 in
(8–10 mm).
Flight season: April–
June and (sometimes)
July–August.
Nectar sources:
Very varied.
Habitat: Woodland,
meadows, parks, gardens.

Nomada goodeniana

Gooden's Nomad Bee

This small, wasp-like bee has a fascinating lifestyle, in some ways reminiscent of a cuckoo, and can be found in Europe. In common with its mining bee hosts, it can often be seen flying over bare ground and short vegetation during the spring. Sometimes, a second generation emerges in the late summer. A female nomad bee will search for the nest tunnel of a mining bee, then sneak in and lay her eggs in the pollen-stocked nest cell of the host. When they hatch, the intruder's larvae have sickle-shaped mouthparts, which they use to destroy the eggs or larvae of the host mining bee—so the young nomad bee gets all the pollen. Such behaviour earns this bee its description as a kleptoparasite.

Adults are mainly hairless and brightly coloured, with bold black and yellow stripes on the abdomen, yellow spots on the black thorax, and orange legs and antennae. They feed on nectar from many flowers, including dandelions, willows, buttercups, ragworts, forget-me-nots, cow parsley, rape, and greater stitchwort, incidentally picking up pollen as they go.

9

Characteristics

Length: 0.26–0.33 in
(6.5–8.5 mm).
Flight season: March–July.
Nectar sources:
Very varied.
Habitat: Heaths,
commons, sandpits.

Andrena barbilabris

Sandpit Mining Bee

These bees visit the flowers of willows, hawthorns, daisies, gorse, and dandelions in spring, and ragwort in summer. Females have a very furry thorax, reddish on top and yellow on the sides, and a yellow head. The shiny, dark abdomen has several narrow stripes of pale hairs running across it. Males appear silvery due to the white hairs on the sides of the thorax. This bee occupies suitable habitat in large parts of central and northern Europe, northern Asia, and North America.

They nest in a burrow in loose, sandy soil, often on footpaths or even in the gaps between paving stones. Many females may nest in close proximity, and large numbers of males may swarm around these aggregations. When a female enters or leaves a nest burrow, she allows the sand to collapse behind her, presumably to conceal its location. This is important because, in Europe, the tiny sandpit blood bee will be looking for any opportunity to take advantage. The blood bee is a kleptoparasite; if it locates a mining bee's nest hole it will burrow down it, open one of its cells, destroy the host egg or larva inside, and lay its own egg there before sealing the cell again and making its escape.

10

Characteristics

Length: 0.47–0.71 in
(12–18 mm).
Flight season:
May–October.
Nectar sources: Various,
including bird's-foot
trefoil.
Habitat: Woodland,
grassland, scrub.

Anthidium oblongatum

Oblong Woolcarder Bee

This robustly built solitary bee is native to Eurasia, but was accidentally introduced to the United States in the 1990s and has since spread across several eastern states, including New York, New Jersey, and Pennsylvania. It looks more like a wasp than a bee. The head and thorax are mainly black, with yellow spots and bars, and the broad, flattened abdomen has bold, broken yellow stripes running across it. The legs are reddish-orange.

Females use their comblike mandibles to comb, or "card," fibers from the leaves and stems of hairy plants such as lamb's-ear, mullein, and yarrow. They use this material to build the walls of brood cells inside their nest burrow, which is usually in a pre-existing cavity in a wall, wood, or the ground; it may be the abandoned burrow of another insect. Females pick up pollen with the specialist hairs on the undersides of their abdomens and feed this and nectar from flowers such as bird's-foot trefoil and vetches to their brood. Unusually for a bee, the males are larger than the females. They are fiercely territorial and have three spines at the tips of their abdomens, which they use as weapons to defend their territory.

11

Unequal Cellophane Bee

Characteristics

Length: Female 0.47–0.51 in (12–13 mm); male 0.35–0.39 in (9–10 mm). Flight season: March–July. Nectar sources: Very varied, including fruit trees. Habitat: Meadows, grassland, riverbanks, parks, gardens.

One of the first pollinators to emerge in spring, the males usually appear first, spending their days visiting apple, cherry, and blueberry flowers, and searching for newly emerged females. These bees have heart-shaped faces, with the eyes slanting downward as the head tapers toward the mouth. The head and thorax are dark, with paler hairs, and the abdomen has ivory-coloured stripes rimmed with pale hairs.

Native to eastern North America, the unequal cellophane bee is one of the plasterer bees, whose name comes from their habit of lining nest cells with a waterproof, fungus-resistant, cellophane-like substance. When dry, it looks like clear plastic. Each cell is filled with a mixture of pollen and nectar, with an egg attached to the upper wall of the cell. The bees collect impressive quantities of pollen from a wide range of flowers on their hind legs. Nests up to 18 in (45 cm) deep are burrowed in light soil, even in urban back gardens. They are called "solitary" bees because each female excavates her own nest, but in suitable conditions there may be hundreds or thousands of burrows in close proximity.

12

Characteristics

Length: 0.31 in (8 mm).
Flight season:
February–November.
Nectar sources:
Flowers from more
than 20 families.
Habitat: Woodland,
farmland, prairies.

Augochlora pura

Gold-green Sweat Bee

Sweat bees are named for their habit of licking perspiration off human skin to obtain minerals. So strikingly iridescent are these gold-green bees that they look like little flying emeralds in sunshine. They are important pollinators, known for visiting more than 20 families of plants in their quest for nectar and pollen. Only the females have pollen-collecting hairs on their hind legs. Emerging early in the year and remaining active late into fall, they are found only in eastern North America, ranging from Florida to southern Quebec.

A female sweat bee builds a nest in moist, rotting wood, often in an abandoned insect burrow. The nest has multiple cells lined with a waxy substance from her wax glands. One egg is laid in each cell, which is stocked with pollen and nectar for the larva when it emerges. The time between an egg being laid and an adult emerging from a pupa varies from 17 to 40 days, depending on latitude, so there are two or three generations each year. Gold-green sweat bees are solitary: one female builds the nest and cares for the young, but it is common for many females to build their nests close together.

13

Characteristics

Length: 0.39–0.43 in
(10–11 mm).
Flight season:
April–October.
Nectar sources:
Very varied.
Habitat: Meadows,
parks, gardens.

Agapostemon virescens

Striped Sweat Bee

Striped sweat bees (also known as bicoloured agapostemons) live in many parts of the United States and southern Canada. They drink nectar at many flowers, including those of Joe Pye weeds, coneflowers, goldenrods, sunflowers, and peas. The bee has a shining, metallic green head and thorax—similar to a gold-green sweat bee—but its abdomen is striped black and yellow (male) or black and white (female). The male has bright-yellow legs. This species is an important pollinator, visiting a wide range of flowers. It builds its nest burrows in the ground, often on a south-facing slope.

This sweat bee is described as a communal bee, neither eusocial nor solitary. That is because one entrance tunnel leads into a network of underground side passages, each dug by one female and each with its own egg cells. One egg is laid in each cell, which has a supply of pollen and nectar for the grub when it hatches. The advantage of this breeding strategy is that, since there may be a number of adult females inside the nest complex at any one time, there is less chance of a kleptoparasitic cuckoo bee gaining entry.

14

Characteristics

Length: 0.39–0.47 in (10–12 mm).
Flight season: March–May.
Nectar sources: Fruit trees.
Habitat: Forest edge, farmland, grassland, gardens.

Osmia lignaria

Blue Orchard Mason Bee

Native to North America, blue orchard mason bees have a metallic, greenish-blue head, thorax, and abdomen. They are exceptional pollinators of fruit trees early in spring. For this reason, they are managed by orchard farmers, who place "bee hotels" made from wooden tubes or simply drill holes in wood near the apples, pears, plums, cherries, peaches, or almonds they want the bees to pollinate. Since these bees don't fly far for their pollen, this is a good way of enticing them to stay close to the orchard.

The males emerge first, feeding and waiting for females to take to the wing. After bee couples have mated, the females go in search of suitable nest holes. Unlike carpenter bees, they can't excavate their own burrows, so they depend on natural cavities—or those put out for them by farmers. A mixture of pollen, nectar, and saliva is rolled into a food ball at the farthest section of the hole, an egg is laid on it, and a cell is sealed with a mud partition. The female builds five to eight cells in the cavity and goes off to do the same again. She may fill several burrows with eggs before she dies. Inside, the eggs hatch, the grubs eat the food ball, and eventually change into pupae—to emerge the following spring as the next generation.

15

Characteristics

Length: Queen 1.38 in
(35 mm); worker
0.98 in (25 mm).
Flight season:
April–November.
Nectar sources: Ivy.
Habitat: Woodland,
grassland,
meadows, gardens.

Vespa crabro

European Hornet

The European hornet has a black-and-yellow head, a red-brown thorax, and an orange-and-brown-striped abdomen. Its large size and brash colours, enhanced by a loud buzz when it flies, give this insect a fearsome appearance, but it is generally a docile insect, less likely to deliver a sting than its smaller common wasp cousin. It will only sting if its nest is threatened. Native to Europe, this large social wasp was introduced to North America in the 1880s. It is a predatory insect, feeding its larvae smaller wasps, flies, and moths, and eating windfall fruit and tree sap. Hornets also visit and pollinate flowers to stock up on nectar before hibernating.

A queen hornet starts nest building in April or May, typically in a dark, hollow tree or under the floor of an outhouse. She mixes saliva and chewed plant fibers to make the "plaster" for cell partitions, into which she lays eggs. These develop into nonbreeding worker hornets, willing helpers who take over the construction of the colony. Later, fertile males and females hatch. These mate after nuptial flights. The females will be the following year's queen hornets, and they go into hibernation, while the males, workers, and old queen perish.

HOVERFLIES AND FLOWER FLIES

Hoverflies, or flower flies, are one of the most important groups of pollinators of agricultural crops, fruit trees, and many flowers, despite the fact that they have no specific pollen-carrying structures. Their attractive black-and-yellow or orange coloration makes them beautiful additions to any garden. The colour schemes also mean they are often mistaken for wasps or bees, and this mimicry is a good defence against predators, which tend to avoid them for fear of being stung. In fact, hoverflies have no stinger. There are about 6,000 different kinds of hoverflies in the family Syrphidae. Like bees and butterflies, they practice complete metamorphosis, with four stages of the life cycle: egg, larva, pupa, and adult. Unlike the former, however, they have two wings, not four.

A hoverfly's command of the air is incredible. As well as hovering, it can fly forward and backward, up and down. Its acceleration from a hovering start is simply breathtaking. The adults feed, mate, and lay eggs. They obtain energy-giving nectar and protein-rich pollen from flowers. Most prefer flowers in which the nectar and pollen are easy to reach, like umbellifers, thistles, and knapweeds. Some, however, have a long snout (rostrum), which they insert into more tubular flowers, such as red campions and bluebells. Others don't visit flowers at all, but feed on the sugary secretions of aphids (honeydew) and pollen grains stuck to the surfaces of leaves. The larvae of some are predatory, feeding on other small invertebrates, such as aphids.

(opposite) Helophilus pendulus *on Michaelmas daisy.*

16

Characteristics

Length: 0.98 in (25 mm).
Flight season:
May–October.
Nectar sources:
Many flowers.
Habitat: Meadows,
forest edge, gardens.

Volucella zonaria

Hornet Mimic Hoverfly

With a wingspan of 1.58 in (40 mm) and a head and body length of 0.98 in (25 mm), this impressive European insect looks like a menacing hornet but is actually a beautiful, harmless hoverfly. It has a yellow face, forehead, and antennae, with reddish-brown compound eyes. The thorax is reddish-brown, and the abdomen orange-yellow with two black bands. The clear wings have an orange tint. The stingless hornet mimic hoverfly is thought to have evolved to imitate the appearance of a more menacing hornet as a warning to predators; this is called Batesian mimicry.

These hoverflies are important pollinators. They nectar at valerians, oregano, buddleia, mint, scabious, thistles, and dogwoods. Females trick sociable wasps by laying eggs in their nests. When they hatch, the larvae have a commensal relationship with their hosts: they clean the nest by eating dead workers and larvae and dropped food, and they receive protection from other predators—which daren't attack a wasp nest! They grow and pupate in the nest, and the following spring the flying adults emerge, probably at night to avoid conflict with the wasps.

17

Characteristics
Length: 0.35–0.47 in
(9–12 mm).
Flight season: All
year on warm days.
Nectar sources:
Many flowers.
Habitat: Meadows,
forest edge, farmland,
scrub, parks, gardens.

Episyrphus balteatus
Marmalade Hoverfly

On warm, sunny days these smart orange-and-black insects can be seen hovering near flowers, their wings a blur of rapid movement, before darting away in the blink of an eye. They collect nectar and pollen from a wide range of flat-topped flowers, such as daisies, ragwort, thistles, and knapweeds. The UK's commonest hoverflies, they also live throughout much of Eurasia and North Africa.

Each segment of the abdomen has dark bands separated by orange bands. If the larvae of a marmalade hoverfly develop in hot conditions, they produce adults with more orange on the abdomen, sometimes almost lacking any black. Conversely, if the grubs grow in cooler weather, the adults will be darker, sometimes almost black. Close examination reveals clear wings with a distinctive pattern of veins, and reddish-brown eyes. If the eyes touch at the top of the head, the hoverfly is a male.

Summer "plagues of wasps" sometimes reported on south and east coasts of England are, in fact, usually migrant marmalade hoverflies arriving from continental Europe. Rather than being harmful, they are beneficial. Not only do the adults pollinate flowers, the larvae eat a range of aphids, including cereal and cabbage aphids.

18

Characteristics

Length: 0.31–0.35 in
(8–9 mm).

Flight season: Mostly
April–September.

Nectar sources: Various,
including fruit trees.

Habitat: Forest, farmland,
orchards, parks, gardens.

Allograpta obliqua

Oblique Stripetail

One of North America's most common hoverflies, the oblique stripetail is delicately marked. It has a yellow face, reddish-brown complex eyes, a dark-brown thorax with yellowish patches on the sides, and black-and-yellow transverse stripes on the first three sections of the abdomen. On the fourth and fifth segments (tergites) of the abdomen, the stripes run at an oblique angle, giving the stripetail its name. The adults are important pollinators of flowers and fruit trees and their grubs are responsible for eating large numbers of the aphid pests of fruit trees and vegetables.

This insect lives in most parts of the United States, southern Canada, Mexico, and islands in the Caribbean. In the southern part of its range it flies all year; farther north, the flight season is shorter. Eggs are laid near aphids; they hatch after two or three days in the south, up to eight days in the north. The newly hatched grubs then set to work eating aphids, mealy bugs, and mites. Research has shown more than 30 can be consumed by a single hoverfly larva daily. After five to fourteen days, the larvae pupate and then take on their flying incarnation.

19

Characteristics

Length: 0.24–0.31 in
(6–8 mm).
Flight season:
April–November.
Nectar sources:
Many flowers.
Habitat: Forest, farmland,
orchards, parks, gardens.

Toxomerus geminatus

Eastern Calligrapher

Sunflowers, fleabanes, and other daisies act as magnets for this hoverfly, which visits them and many other blooms in search of nectar. Its serial visitations to flowers ensure the transfer of pollen from one to another. Like many other hoverflies, adult eastern calligraphers are coloured and patterned to trick predators into thinking they are predatory wasps and bees. However, they don't have a stinger and are completely harmless. The eastern calligrapher has a yellow face, reddish-brown eyes, a brown-and-yellow thorax, and a black-and-yellow patterned abdomen. Rather than simple stripes, the black is intricately shaped, with zigzag margins and an anchor pattern, as if finely worked by a calligrapher.

The eastern calligrapher is one of the most common hoverflies in eastern North America, its range extending from southern Canada to Texas and Florida. Its western equivalent lives in the Pacific coast states of the continent. Adults can be seen on the wing anywhere there are flattish-topped flowers; it can't feed in tubular ones. As well as nectar and pollen, it feeds on aphids' honeydew. Unlike its own larvae, however, an adult doesn't have the mouthparts needed to prey upon the aphids themselves.

20

Length: 0.55–0.71 in
(14–18 mm).
Flight season: March–June.
Nectar sources:
Many flowers.
Habitat: Forest edge,
meadows, scrub, gardens.

Bombylius major

Large Bee Fly

With its very hairy, orange-buff body and beelike flight, this insect fools most people into thinking it's a bumblebee. Many birds, and other predators, are fooled too! This kind of mimicry serves the bee fly very well. Like other flies, it has two wings, but it is not a typical fly. It has a very long, rigid proboscis, ideal for drinking nectar as it hovers in front of a flower. And its wings are two-toned, the front part blackish and the rear clear.

Bee flies live in temperate Eurasia and North America. They are effective pollinators of early-flowering plants, but their predatory larvae limit the populations of other species of pollinators. They are parasitic insects. Female bee flies lay their eggs close to the nests of solitary bees and wasps. When the larvae hatch, they find their way into the nest burrow of their host and do untold damage—not only eating the food stored by the parent bee or wasp, but eating the host's larvae as well.

BUTTERFLIES AND MOTHS

Although their role is often ignored, many of the 180,000 species of butterflies and moths (collectively making up the insect order Lepidoptera) are important pollinators. Butterflies fly by day and include some of the most beautiful and brightly coloured insects. Many moths are also active by day, but most are strictly nocturnal. The wings and bodies of butterflies and moths are covered with tiny scales, which give them their coloration. The vast majority have four wings and drink nectar using a long proboscis.

All practice complete metamorphosis, with eggs hatching into larvae, or caterpillars, then becoming pupae before emerging as flying adults. The female lays eggs on a host plant, which becomes a food plant when the caterpillars hatch. They are "eating machines" and some damage crops. Some butterflies and moths are very choosy about the plant they lay their eggs on; if that plant isn't present in an area, neither will be the butterfly. Other species lay on a wide range of plants. After pupation, the next generation of adults emerges. Many butterflies and moths visit flowers to collect nectar and in so doing they unwittingly transfer pollen and facilitate pollination. They tend not to be so fussy with their nectar requirements as their caterpillars are with feeding needs. Some don't eat at all, relying on stored fat and flying for only a short time.

*(opposite) Clouded yellow (*Colias croceus*) nectaring.*

21

Characteristics

Wingspan: 1.77–2.76 in
(45–70 mm).
Flight season:
May–October.
Nectar sources:
Very varied.
Habitat: Open areas
with bare ground.

Junonia coenia

Common Buckeye

With its wings spread, this is a stunning butterfly. Each brown forewing has a large and a small eyespot—presumably to deter predators—and two orange bars. Each hind wing, also mostly brown, has another two eyespots. The females are larger than the males. Buckeyes are resident in the Deep South of the United States and in much of Mexico, with adults from the year's first brood migrating north in late spring to temporarily colonize regions to the north, as far as southern Canada east of the Rockies and northern California to the west.

Adults are attracted to a wide range of flowers to feed on nectar, including thistles, chickory, gumweed, knapweed, and sunflowers. Males perch on low vegetation or bare earth, on the lookout for passing females. After mating, females lay eggs singly on the top of the leaves or leaf buds of plants such as false foxgloves, toadflax, and plantains, which the caterpillars will eat later. Several generations are produced each year. Caterpillars and adults overwinter in the south but cannot survive the winter farther north.

Speyeria cybele

Great Spangled Fritillary

Characteristics

Wingspan: 2.44–3.46 in
(62–88 mm).
Flight season:
June–September.
Nectar sources:
Very varied.
Habitat: Open, moist
meadows and
open woodland.

This large, fast-flying, yet easily approachable butterfly is the most common fritillary in most of eastern North America. The upperwings are bright orange with bold black bars and spots creating a particularly striking appearance. When the wings are closed, the underwing pattern can be seen, showing areas of red-brown and pale orange, with white spots and black marks. The females are larger and darker than the males. Great spangled fritillaries range from Arkansas and Georgia in the south to Alberta and Nova Scotia in Canada; west of the Rockies, they live from California to British Columbia.

Adults nectar on a variety of flowers when they emerge, typically in mid-June. Milkweeds, passionflowers, coneflowers, thistles, ironweed, dogbane, and mountain laurel are all preferred. Males fly in search of females, and in late summer eggs are laid on, or near, violets. Unusually, the caterpillars do not feed when they emerge, but remain in situ through the winter, feasting at night on young violet leaves the following spring. There is just one generation each year.

23

Characteristics

Wingspan: 2.28–2.91 in
(58–74 mm).
Flight season:
April–October.
Nectar sources:
Very varied.
Habitat: Heaths, meadows,
farmland, parks, gardens.

Vanessa cardui

Painted Lady

The orange, black, and white upperwings of this medium-sized butterfly are distinctive. This is the world's most widespread butterfly, found on every continent except Australia and Antarctica, although it is a year-round resident only in the warmer regions. Large numbers—sometimes many millions—migrate north and west from North Africa and the Middle East each spring, reaching as far northwest as Iceland. The longest migrations may be 9,320 miles (15,000 km). Similar northward movements take place in North America, where the butterfly is also known as the "cosmopolitan," with painted ladies flying from Mexico into the United States and southern Canada.

The adults are not fussy feeders, visiting flowers of over 300 species of plants in search of nectar; thistles are particularly sought after. They also eat aphid honeydew. Males are territorial, waiting for females to enter their territory before engaging in courtship. Mating takes place throughout the year, including during migration, during which several generations may be produced. Females lay around 500 eggs, each laid singly on a host plant, commonly thistle, hollyhock, mallow, or milkweed.

24

Characteristics
Wingspan: 3.5–4 in
(89–102 mm).
Flight season: All year in
southern United States.
Nectar sources: Milkweeds.
Habitat: Meadows,
farmland, roadside verges.

Danaus plexippus

Monarch

The monarch is renowned for its bright appearance and long migratory flights. It is one of the best-known butterflies, even among people who have never seen one in the wild. The male's upperwings are bright orange, those of the female orange-brown. Both sexes have wide black borders and veins, the black borders spotted with white. Monarch populations in tropical regions are mostly resident, but at higher latitudes they are migrants. In fall, millions migrate from the eastern United States and southern Canada to central Mexico, where they roost in trees during the winter and become active on warm days to fly in search of nectar.

In spring, most migrant monarchs mate before setting off on long journeys that will take some as far north as Canada. The females lay eggs singly under the leaves of milkweeds along the way. These are also their preferred nectar flowers, but early in the season, before they bloom, monarchs visit lilacs, red clover, thistles, and dogbane. There may be up to six broods in Mexico and the southern United States, perhaps just one in the far north of their range.

25

Characteristics

Wingspan: 3.27–3.98 in
(83–101 mm).
Flight season: All year.
Nectar sources: Lantanas
and fruit trees.
Habitat: Forests
and orchards.

Siproeta stelenes
Malachite

Named for the green mineral of the same name, the malachite is a truly beautiful butterfly, whose upperwings sport spots and larger patches of translucent pale green on dark brown or black. The underwings are pale green, rufous-brown, and cream. The trailing edges of the wings are scalloped. This species is native to tropical South and Central America and Caribbean islands, but Cuban-based malachites colonized southern Florida in the 1960s, and there are now established populations there and in Texas. Individuals sometimes wander into other southern states. In the tropics, this is a forest butterfly, but in Florida it breeds in mango, citrus, and avocado orchards.

Males remain motionless on trees for long periods, periodically going in search of females with a slow, floating flight where dappled sunlight shines through the tree canopy. Females lay their eggs singly on the underside of leaves, particularly those of wild petunias. Adults go to roost in late afternoon, often gathering in groups on the underside of leaves. Although the adults' main food is rotting fruit, this species is also an important pollinator, visiting the flowers of trees, including fruit trees and lianas.

26

Characteristics

Wingspan: 3–3.5 in
(76–88 mm).
Flight season:
March–October.
Nectar sources: Willows,
scabious, and knapweeds.
Habitat: Open woodland,
forest edge, parks, gardens.

Nymphalis antiopa

Mourning Cloak

With its deep-maroon-red upperwings, bordered with cream or white, and with a row of blue spots, the mourning cloak is unmistakeable. Its underwings are gray or brown, bordered white, and the sexes are alike. The first two specimens of this beautiful butterfly to be described were found at Camberwell, London, in 1748. Sadly the species is only an occasional visitor to the UK, where it is known as the Camberwell beauty. Native to northern Eurasia and North America, in Europe some populations migrate south in fall.

In parts of Scandinavia or southern Canada, these are the first butterflies to be seen in early spring. They may emerge from hibernation while snow is still lying on the ground and before trees have come into bud. Since the adults feed mostly on tree sap and rotting fruit, their role as pollinators is not as great as many other butterflies, but they can sometimes be seen nectaring at willow or knapweed flowers. The caterpillars eat the leaves of willows, elms, hackberries, and hawthorns.

27

Characteristics

Wingspan: 2–2.5 in
(50–64 mm).
Flight season: Mostly
March–October.
Nectar sources:
Very varied.
Habitat: Forest glades,
woodland edge, gardens.

Polygonia c-album

Comma

The comma's flight is characteristic: short glides on its bright-orange wings between series of wingbeats. In flight, it is easy to see, but at rest, on browning bracken or a tree trunk, the jagged outline of its wings gives the superficial appearance of a dead leaf. This camouflage offers some protection from predators. A white comma-shaped mark on the underside of the hind wing gives this European butterfly its name. Preferred nectar flowers include thistles, brambles, ivy, knapweeds, and privet.

Adults emerge from hibernation on warm days in early spring. Males establish territories, returning time and again to the same perch, perhaps in a woodland glade, after making short flights to investigate passing females. After mating, the females find a suitable site—often a patch of nettles—on which to lay their eggs. Later, the hatched caterpillars munch their way through countless nettles, pupate, and emerge as beautiful adults in early summer. Another generation is produced in late summer or early fall. Adults on the wing in fall stock up on nectar from a variety of flowers, pollinating as they go. At this time of year, they are more likely to visit gardens, even in cities.

28

Characteristics
Wingspan: 2.5–3 in
(63–75 mm).
Flight season: Mostly
March–October.
Nectar sources: Many
common flowers.
Habitat: Meadows, open
woodland, forest glades,
suburban gardens, heaths.

Aglais io

Peacock

The gray-and-black underwings of a peacock butterfly render it inconspicuous when its wings are closed. It could pass as a dead leaf and will be ignored by most predators. If a small bird is about to attack, however, it will open its wings, exposing the rusty red and four dazzling yellow, blue, and black eyespots on its upperwings—and give itself a chance to escape. This very mobile butterfly can be seen in much of Eurasia in a very broad range of habitats; it often visits back gardens, even in cities. And, unlike many butterflies, its range seems to be expanding.

Adults spend most of the morning nectaring at thistles, betony, bluebells, hawkweeds, ragwort, yarrow, and many other flowers. Although males and females look alike, they behave differently. Around the middle of the day, males become territorial, seeking out passing females. If a female does mate, she will later lay her eggs in clusters of up to 400 on the underside of nettle leaves. Peacocks hibernate in the winter and are sometimes disturbed from sheltered places such as backyard sheds.

29

Characteristics

Wingspan: 2.25–3 in (57–78 mm).
Flight season: All year in the south; August–September in the north.
Nectar sources: Tubular flowers.
Habitat: Fields, scrub, gardens, parks.

Phoebis sennae

Cloudless Sulphur

This bright-yellow butterfly is a permanent resident in much of South and Central America and the southern United States; it also strays north and may breed as far north as the Great Lakes. Males have lemon-yellow upper- and underwings, while females can be paler and have a dark spot in the middle of the forewing. In both sexes, the underside of the hind wings has two pink-edged silvery spots. Although brightly coloured, cloudless sulphurs can "disappear" against a background of pale leaves, a useful protection against predatory birds.

Males make dashing flights around nectar plants in search of receptive females. They have relatively long tongues, so can reach the nectaries of tubular flowers that many other butterflies cannot. These include morning glories, bougainvilleas, lantanas, and cardinal flowers. Females are more selective in their choice of host plants on which to lay their eggs, targeting various species of peas. Cloudless sulphurs fly year-round in the far south of the United States, but migrants to the north of the country may be seen only in August and September. Their southbound migration in fall may be more noticeable than that of monarchs.

30

Characteristics

Wingspan: 3–4 in
(76–102 mm).
Flight season:
February–November.
Nectar sources:
Very varied.
Habitat: Deciduous forest,
swampy forest, gardens.

Papilio troilus

Spicebush Swallowtail

This spectacular New World species is found in damp forests and swamplands throughout the southeast of the United States and in southern Ontario. Larger than its Old World cousin (which also lives in North America), it has blackish-brown forewings with white spots along the trailing edges. The hind wings have a coloured half-moon, which can be dazzling in sunlight; this is greenish-blue in males and bright blue in females. And, of course, each hind wing sports a long "tail." Joe Pye weed, jewelweed, honeysuckle, thistles, milkweed, and dogbane are all visited for nectar.

If a male spicebush swallowtail sees a female, he will perform slow courtship flights, hovering above his potential partner. The female lays her eggs on the leaves of a host plant. When they hatch, the newly emerged caterpillars set about feasting and growing. Pupation takes place near the ground. In Florida and along the Gulf Coast, there are at least three generations each year, with only two farther north. In common with many other butterflies, these swallowtails can be seen "puddling"— gathering around a puddle, sometimes in large numbers, to collect moisture and minerals from damp soil.

31

Characteristics

Wingspan: 3–3.27 in
(76–83 mm).
Flight season:
March–September.
Nectar sources: Many,
including knapweeds
and thistles.
Habitat: Meadows,
prairies, farmland,
parks, gardens.

Papilio machaon

Old World Swallowtail

This large, colourful butterfly is a strong, fast flyer and an important pollinator. The forewings are creamy yellow with dark-gray, veinlike markings and black patches. Each of the hind wings has a "tail," circular blue marks along the border, and a small red eyespot; the eyespots almost touch when the wings are held open. The species is found widely in Eurasia, from tropical regions to the far north of Scandinavia, and—despite its name—in North America. In the UK, it is restricted to the Fens, where its caterpillars feed only on milk parsley. Migrants from continental Europe sometimes appear in southern England.

Swallowtails drink nectar from angelicas, knapweeds, thistles, red campions, valerians, and flag irises. While nectaring, they often flutter their wings, a characteristic of members of the Papilionidae family. Females lay their eggs singly, and they hatch into pale-green caterpillars with black stripes and orange dots. There are two or three generations annually. If the last eggs are laid too late to allow adult emergence before the coming winter, the pupae will overwinter.

32

Characteristics

Wingspan: 1.18–1.58 in
(30–40 mm).
Flight season:
May–September.
Nectar sources:
Horseshoe vetch.
Habitat:
Limestone grassland.

Polyomattus bellargus

Adonis Blue

The Adonis blue has very specific habitat requirements and an extraordinary lifestyle. It likes sunny, well-drained south-facing slopes on chalk or limestone grassland where horseshoe vetch grows. It nectars on the yellow flowers of this plant, and its caterpillars feed on the plant's leaves. Male Adonis blues can be seen flying low to the ground, their brilliant sky-blue upperwings flashing in the sunlight. Females are less conspicuous because they fly less frequently and their upperwings are chocolate-brown. Both species have ocher underwings dappled with orange, black, and white spots. Since they are colonial butterflies, on hot sunny days many can sometimes be seen in the same small area of grassland. They are found in suitable habitats in western Asia and Europe, including the chalk hills of southern England.

Adonis blues overwinter as caterpillars, which are attended by ants that come to feed from sugary secretions they produce. As a trade-off, the ants provide protection from predators. The caterpillars metamorphose in small hollows on the ground near ants' nests, and the ants bury them under a layer of soil—giving more protection. The year's first generation of adults emerges in May, with a second generation in July.

33

Characteristics
Wingspan: 1.58–1.97 in
(40–50 mm).
Flight season: All
year on warm days.
Nectar sources:
Honeysuckle, red
valerian, jasmine, lilac.
Habitat: Meadows,
woodland edge,
park, gardens.

Macroglossum stellatarum

Hummingbird Hawk-moth

At first glimpse, the sight of this remarkable little moth hovering at a honeysuckle or jasmine flower is reminiscent of a hummingbird. Its incredibly fast-beating wings produce an audible hum, and its very long proboscis is ideal for nectaring at flowers with long corollae. This is primarily a day-flying species, though it is sometimes active at night. Its forewings are brown and it has orange hind wings. The abdomen is broad and its "tail" can be spread like that of a hummingbird to aid maneuverability in flight. These hawk-moths have learnt to take full advantage of well-stocked flowerbeds so they are frequently seen in gardens.

Humingbird hawk-moths live in much of Europe and parts of North Africa and western Asia. Most of the ones seen in the UK are migrants from continental Europe, but some are resident, hibernating over winter in crevices in trees and outbuildings. They emerge to nectar on warm days, even in winter. Later, females lay their eggs on bedstraws, the food plants of the caterpillars.

34

Characteristics

Wingspan: 2.56–3.55 in (65–90 mm).
Flight season: February–November.
Nectar sources: Columbines, evening primrose, honeysuckle, lilac, clovers, thistles
Habitats: Scrub, gardens, meadows, deserts.

Hyles lineata

White-lined Sphinx

This North American moth is a member of the Sphingidae, the same family as the hawk-moths. It has long, tapering wings and hovers like a hummingbird at nectar flowers. The sphinx moth feeds mostly at dusk and through the night, but sometimes during the day as well. As a by-product of this activity, it is an important pollinator of columbines, evening primrose, honeysuckle, lilac, clover, and thistles. The forewing is dark brown, with a pale stripe extending from the base to the apex. A broad pink band runs across the hind wing. Black and white stripes run across the abdomen.

Females attract males by releasing pheromones, which the latter can detect even when far away. After mating, the females lay eggs on host plants. The caterpillars come in a range of colours. They eat voraciously—making them unpopular with some farmers and gardeners—then burrow into the soil when they are ready to pupate. After two or three weeks, they wriggle to the surface and the next generation emerges. In the warm climate of Mexico and the southern United States, there are usually several generations every year.

35

Hemaris diffinis

Snowberry Clearwing

With its transparent wings, this swift-flying pollinator of the eastern United States looks more like a bumblebee than a moth. In fact, it is sometimes known as the bumblebee moth. Its thorax is olive-gold, and the abdomen is black and yellow, but its clear wings with black veins and a reddish-brown border are the moth's most striking feature. Pollen becomes attached to hairs on the moth's body as it visits flowers to drink nectar using its long proboscis. Popular nectar givers include lantanas, honeysuckles, snowberries, thistles, and lilacs.

Once the first adult clearwings emerge from cocoons in May or June, there is no break in activity. After mating, females lay their eggs on snowberries, honeysuckles, or dogbane. Green caterpillars hatch, then eat and grow for about a month, passing through several stages or instars before pupating in cocoons spun in leaf litter on the ground. Later, the summer's second generation of adults takes to the wing and the cycle repeats, with their young overwintering as pupae.

36

Characteristics

Wingspan: 1.65–2 in
(42–52 mm).
Flight season:
July–September.
Nectar sources:
Buddleia, thistles, and
many other flowers.
Habitat: Gardens,
parks, waste ground,
coastal scrub.

Euplagia quadripunctaria

Jersey Tiger Moth

Despite the bold black-and-white pattern of its forewings, a Jersey tiger moth can be inconspicuous when perched. When it takes to the wing, however, its orange hind wings flash brightly. Follow the movement to the moth's next flower perch and you will be rewarded with good views, because this is an approachable species when feeding. A closer look reveals small yellow patches on the forewings and black blotches on the hind wings. These moths feed at night, and by day when it is warm, visiting a variety of flowers to drink nectar, including buddleia and thistles. As they travel around, they unwittingly transfer pollen from plant to plant.

A widespread moth in continental Europe, until recently its range in the UK was limited to parts of the south coast. However, it has recently expanded its range and can now be seen in gardens and on wasteland in London and much of southern England. The bright-orange, black, and white caterpillars hatch in September and do not pupate until the following spring. They feed and overwinter on nettles, bramble, ground ivy, and borage.

BEETLES

Some of the most beautiful pollinators are beetles. With at least 400,000 species worldwide, they are the most diverse group. With so many different types, it is not surprising that beetles feature a bewildering array of shapes, colours, and lifestyles. Some are camouflaged to blend into the background, but others are brightly coloured. Many are predators, while those that eat pollen, nectar, or the flowers themselves are important pollinators. Some have a close relationship with just one group of flowers, while others are generalists.

Beetles aren't celebrated as pollinators in the way that bees are, but they were actually performing the role long before any bees, butterflies, and moths. Typical of other insects, beetles have six legs and a three-part body: head, thorax, and abdomen. Their life stages are typical, too, with complete metamorphosis from egg to larva, pupa, and adult. What distinguishes adult beetles is that the front pair of wings is hardened into wing covers, or elytra.

(opposite) Rose chafer beetle (Cetonia aurata).

37

Length: 0.24–0.31 in
(6–8 mm).
Flight season:
March–October.
Nectar sources:
Many flowers.
Habitat: Forest edge,
meadows, parks, gardens.

Anatis mali

Seven-spotted Ladybug

Everyone is familiar with bright, shiny, red ladybugs, and most gardeners know that they are "friends" because of their voracious appetite for aphids. What is less well known is that they also eat nectar and pollen, so play a role in pollinating many plants. The seven-spotted ladybug (or ladybird) is one of about 6,000 species. It is native to Eurasia and has become established in North America, having been introduced to tackle aphid populations. It has a tiny black head, a black thorax with two white spots, and seven black spots on its red wing covers, or elytra. The bright coloration is off-putting for predators, and ladybugs can also emit a foul-tasting fluid when threatened.

The seven-spotted ladybug's reputation as an aphid-killer is not exaggerated. Its eggs are laid near aphid colonies, and when they hatch, the larvae eat about 500 aphids each in the three or four weeks before they pupate. After pupation, adults eat another 5,000 each. In fall, the year's new generation of adults finds a suitable place to overwinter—in a hollow plant stem or under tree bark—ready to emerge again the following spring.

38

Characteristics

Length: 0.31–0.39 in
(8–10 mm).
Flight season:
April–September.
Nectar sources:
Many flowers.
Habitat: Meadows,
scrub, gardens.

Oedemera nobilis

Swollen-thighed Beetle

The flowerheads of oxeye daisies, cornflowers, roses, cow parsley, and brambles are particular favourites of this bright beetle as it feeds on pollen. Readily attracted to gardens by careful planting, it is a productive pollinator. In bright sunlight, the swollen-thighed beetle positively glistens. Its head, thorax, and long, narrow abdomen are metallic green, the wing covers not quite meeting in the middle. Its antennae are noticeably long. The swollen thighs (femora) of the male's hind legs are very obvious, but these are absent in females.

Also known as the thick-legged flower beetle or false oil beetle, this species is common in southern England and also lives in much of Europe and parts of North Africa. Its larvae develop on the dry stems of plants such as thistles, but it is not known whether they overwinter as larvae or pupae. Adults emerge in spring, find mates, and breed.

39

Characteristics

Length: 0.59–0.79 in
(15–20 mm).
Flight season: Late
April–September.
Nectar sources:
Many flowers.
Habitat: Woodland,
scrub, parks, gardens.

Rutpela maculata

Spotted Longhorn Beetle

Also known as the black-and-yellow longhorn, this colourful beetle is usually seen nectaring on the flowerheads of plants such as cow parsley, hogweeds, thistles, and hawthorns. It is wary of disturbance and readily flies when approached. These beetles are common in the UK and across much of Europe, frequenting woodland edge, scrub, parks, and gardens where its food plants grow. The abdomen and wing covers are long and narrow, the latter yellow or orange-yellow with black bands and spots. Some individuals are all black, others all yellow. The front two pairs of legs are yellow, and the hind legs are black.

Spotted longhorns mate on flowers, the female then laying her eggs in decaying fallen timber or rotting stumps, especially of birch trees. This is a long-lived beetle, its complete life cycle lasting two or three years. Most of this time is spent as a grub, which develops within the moist, decaying wood. When it has grown sufficiently, it pupates, emerging as an adult sometime between late April and July. The adults live for four weeks at most.

40

Characteristics

Length: 0.67–0.79 in
(17–20 mm).
Flight season:
May–October.
Nectar source: Dog
rose, brambles.
Habitat: Scrub,
meadows, gardens.

Cetonia aurata

Rose Chafer

The rose chafer lives unseen for most of its life. For two years, it is an unattractive cream-coloured grub, burrowing its way through rotting timber or compost. There, it plays a useful role as a detritivore, recycling the decaying vegetation. After metamorphosis, it spends the following winter as a pupa, then undergoes its final transformation to a brilliantly iridescent, fast-flying beetle. The wing covers, head, and thorax are metallic copper-green, with some fine creamy-white streaks on the covers.

Its coloration makes this insect hard to spot on leaves but very obvious on the petals of a dog rose or bramble flower, where it may be seen feeding on pollen or nectar—or mating—on warm, sunny days. After mating, females lay eggs in rotting wood. Adults live for six to twelve months. Another rose chafer is native to North America, but that is a duller green in colour.

Acknowledgements

The author would like to thank Steven Falk, author of the *Field Guide to the Bees of Great Britain and Ireland* (Bloomsbury 2015), for sharing his expertise on nomad bees.

Picture Credits

All photographs from Shutterstock.
HK-PHOTOGRAPHY (honeybee, front cover left); photomatz (flying honeybees, front cover top); Nejron Photo (butterfly, front cover centre); Scorpp (ladybug, front cover right); V.Borisov (back cover left); irin-k (back cover middle left); Paul Whorton (back cover middle right); T.Irina (back cover right); Dave Massey (pp. 2-3); gary powell (p. 6); thatmacroguy (p. 9); colin robert varndell (p. 41); Shubhrojyoti (p. 53); mar_chm1982 (p. 87).
Plates: Ant Cooper (1); Elliotte Rusty Harold (2); Paul Reeves Photography (3); grynold (4); Unicorn555 (5); ASakoulis (6); Elliotte Rusty Harold (7); Ed Phillips (8); Gabi Wolf (9); Elliotte Rusty Harold (10); Paul Reeves Photography (11); Arto Hakola (12); Paul Reeves Photography (13); Jennifer Bosvert (14); COULANGES (15); aabeele (16); Kletr (17); Darian Williams (18); Elliotte Rusty Harold (19); Bildagentur Zoonar GmbH (20); Steven Russell Smith Ohio (21); Steven Russell Smith Ohio (22); RudiErnst (23); Kate Besler (24); Sue Bishop (25); Glenn Highcove (26); IanRedding (27); Violetta Honkisz (28); Leena Robinson (29); Frode Jacobsen (30); David Havel (31); Martin Fowler (32); Tompi (33); Sari ONeal (34); Brian Lasenby (35); Radka Palenikova (36); Pavel_Voitukovic (37); Sandra Standbridge (38); Jaione_Garcia (39); Sandra Standbridge (40).